I0786776

Toddler Behavior Notes

Parenting toddlers, terrible twos, tantrums/discipline

© 2018 Natalie White

All Rights Reserved

ISBN-13:
978-1719562607

ISBN-10:
1719562601

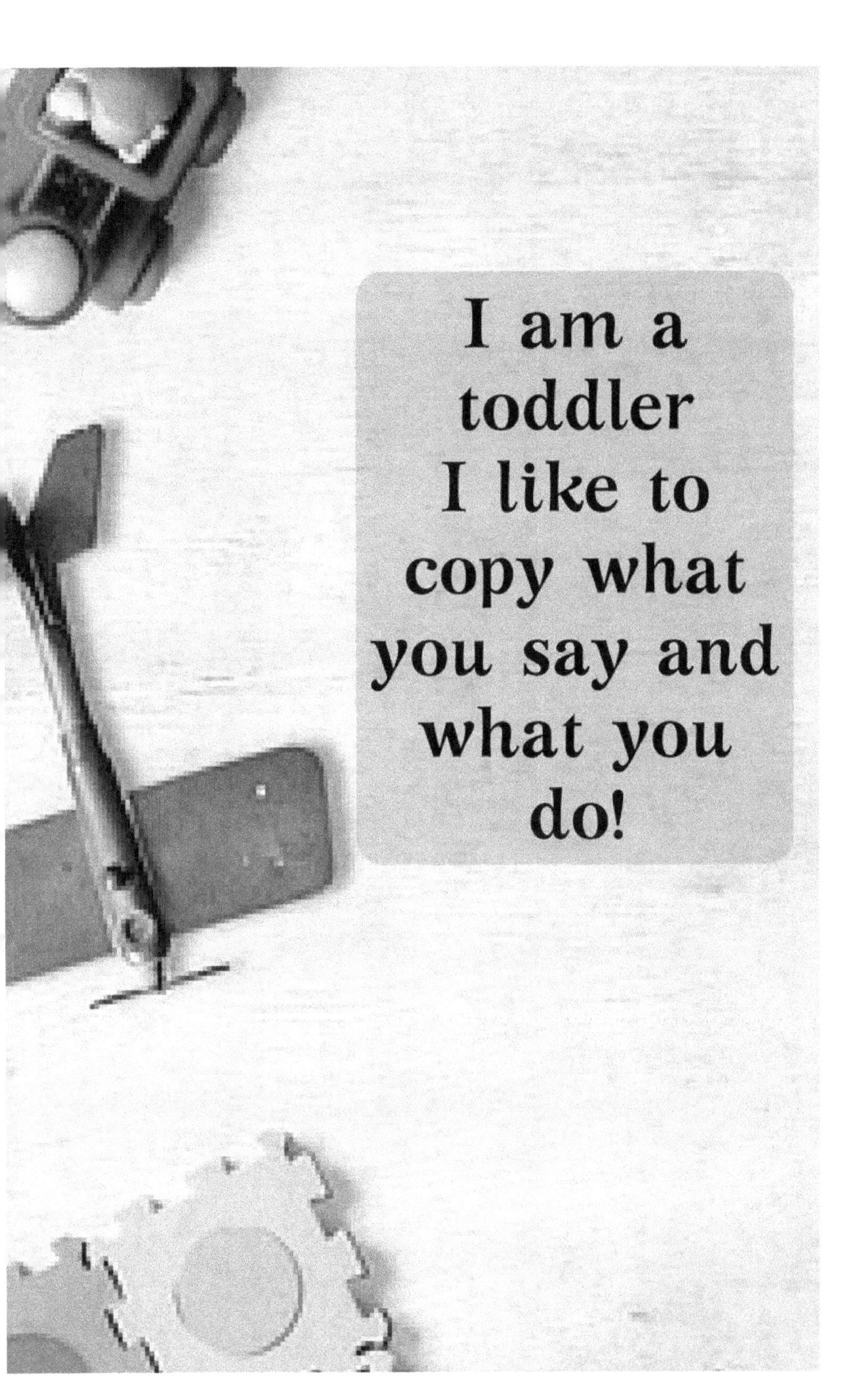
I am a
toddler
I like to
copy what
you say and
what you
do!

Allow me to explore!

Read me stories
For quiet times
Imagination &
dreams

Date: _______________   (Toddler)

Food Eaten:
Breakfast ____
Snack   ____
Lunch   ____
Snack   ____
Dinner   ____
Snack   ____

Drinks: 🥛   1   2   3   4   5   6   7   8

Comments: supplements,(allergies e.t.c)

Sleep: Activities
  Awake:
  Hours sleep last night:
  Nap:
  Asleep:
Poo:
                              Weight   Height
  Times:

Comments, (appearance, unusual smell, straining)

Behavior:

Comments (tiredness, hitting, biting, screaming etc.)

Date:

Parent/Carer

Food Eaten:
  Breakfast _______________________________
  Snack   _______________________________
  Lunch   _______________________________
  Snack   _______________________________
  Dinner   _______________________________
  Snack   _______________________________

Drinks: 1   2   3   4   5   6   7   8   9   10

Comments: supplements,(allergies e.t.c)

Sleep:
  Awake: Activities   To do
  Nap:
  Asleep:

  I feel ...

Most enjoyable moment today...

Parent/carer & toddler activity for tomorrow

Date: [ ]   (Toddler)

Food Eaten:
Breakfast ___________________________________
Snack   ___________________________________
Lunch   ___________________________________
Snack   ___________________________________
Dinner   ___________________________________
Snack   ___________________________________

Drinks: [glass]   1   2   3   4   5   6   7   8

Comments: supplements,(allergies e.t.c)

Sleep: Activities
  Awake:
  Hours sleep last night:
  Nap:
  Asleep:
  Poo:
    Times: [ ] [ ] [ ]   Weight   Height

Comments, (appearance, unusual smell, straining)

Behavior:

Comments (tiredness, hitting, biting, screaming etc.)

Date:

Food Eaten:
   Breakfast _______________________________
   Snack   _______________________________
   Lunch   _______________________________
   Snack   _______________________________
   Dinner   _______________________________
   Snack   _______________________________

Parent/Carer

Drinks: 1   2   3   4   5   6   7 8 9 10

Comments: supplements,(allergies e.t.c)

Sleep:
   Awake:
   Nap:
   Asleep:

Activities

To do

I feel ...

Most enjoyable moment today...

Parent/carer & toddler activity for tomorrow

Date:

(Toddler)

Food Eaten:
Breakfast _______________________________________
Snack   _______________________________________
Lunch   _______________________________________
Snack   _______________________________________
Dinner   _______________________________________
Snack   _______________________________________

Drinks:
1   2   3   4   5   6   7   8

Comments: supplements,(allergies e.t.c)

Sleep: Activities
  Awake:
  Hours sleep last night:
  Nap:
  Asleep:
  Poo:
                              Weight   Height
    Times:

Comments, (appearance, unusual smell, straining)

Behavior:

Comments (tiredness, hitting, biting, screaming etc.)

Date:

Parent/Carer

Food Eaten:
  Breakfast _______________________________
  Snack   _______________________________
  Lunch   _______________________________
  Snack   _______________________________
  Dinner   _______________________________
  Snack   _______________________________

Drinks: 1 2 3 4 5 6 7 8 9 10

Comments: supplements,(allergies e.t.c)

Sleep:
  Awake:
  Nap:
  Asleep:

Activities

To do

I feel ...

Most enjoyable moment today...

Parent/carer & toddler activity for tomorrow

Date: ______   （Toddler）

Food Eaten:
Breakfast ____
Snack   ____
Lunch   ____
Snack   ____
Dinner   ____
Snack   ____

Drinks: 🥛   1   2   3   4   5   6   7   8

Comments: supplements,(allergies e.t.c)

Sleep: Activities
   Awake:
   Hours sleep last night:
   Nap:
   Asleep:
Poo:
                                     Weight   Height
   Times:

Comments, (appearance, unusual smell, straining)

Behavior:

Comments (tiredness, hitting, biting, screaming etc.)

Date:

Parent/Carer

Food Eaten:

Breakfast ______________________________

Snack   ______________________________

Lunch   ______________________________

Snack   ______________________________

Dinner   ______________________________

Snack   ______________________________

Drinks: 1 2 3 4 5 6 7 8 9 10

Comments: supplements,(allergies e.t.c)

Sleep:

Awake:

Nap:

Asleep:

Activities

To do

I feel ...

Most enjoyable moment today...

Parent/carer & toddler activity for tomorrow

Date: [ ]

Toddler

Food Eaten:

Breakfast ___________________________________

Snack   ___________________________________

Lunch   ___________________________________

Snack   ___________________________________

Dinner   ___________________________________

Snack   ___________________________________

Drinks: 1   2   3   4   5   6   7   8

Comments: supplements,(allergies e.t.c)

Sleep: **Activities**

Awake:

Hours sleep last night:

Nap:

Asleep:

Poo:

  Times: Weight   Height

Comments, (appearance, unusual smell, straining)

Behavior:

Comments (tiredness, hitting, biting, screaming etc.)

Date: [ ]

Toddler

Food Eaten:

Breakfast ___________________________________

Snack ___________________________________

Lunch ___________________________________

Snack ___________________________________

Dinner ___________________________________

Snack ___________________________________

Drinks: 1 2 3 4 5 6 7 8

Comments: supplements,(allergies e.t.c)

Sleep:

Awake:

Hours sleep last night:

Nap:

Asleep:

Poo:

Times:

Activities

Weight   Height

Comments, (appearance, unusual smell, straining)

Behavior:

Comments (tiredness, hitting, biting, screaming etc.)

Date:

Food Eaten:

Breakfast ___________________________________

Snack ___________________________________

Lunch ___________________________________

Snack ___________________________________

Dinner ___________________________________

Snack ___________________________________

Drinks: 1   2   3   4   5   6   7   8   9   10

Comments: supplements,(allergies e.t.c)

Parent/Carer

Sleep:

Awake:

Nap:

Asleep:

Activities

To do

I feel ...

Most enjoyable moment today...

Parent/carer & toddler activity for tomorrow

Date: ___________   Toddler

Food Eaten:

Breakfast __________________________________

Snack   __________________________________

Lunch   __________________________________

Snack   __________________________________

Dinner   __________________________________

Snack   __________________________________

Drinks: 1 2 3 4 5 6 7 8

Comments: supplements,(allergies e.t.c)

Sleep: Activities

Awake:

Hours sleep last night:

Nap:

Asleep:

Poo:
                              Weight   Height
Times:

Comments, (appearance, unusual smell, straining,

Behavior:

Comments (tiredness, hitting, biting, screaming etc.)

Date:

Food Eaten:

Breakfast ____________________________________

Snack ____________________________________

Lunch ____________________________________

Snack ____________________________________

Dinner ____________________________________

Snack ____________________________________

Drinks:

1 2 3 4 5 6 7 8 9 10

Parent/Carer

Comments: supplements,(allergies e.t.c)

Sleep:
Awake:
Nap:
Asleep:

Activities

To do

I feel ...

Most enjoyable moment today...

Parent/carer & toddler activity for tomorrow

Date: _________

Toddler

Food Eaten:

Breakfast ______________________________

Snack   ______________________________

Lunch   ______________________________

Snack   ______________________________

Dinner   ______________________________

Snack   ______________________________

Drinks: 1   2   3   4   5   6   7   8

Comments: supplements,(allergies e.t.c)

Sleep:

Awake:

Hours sleep last night:

Nap:

Asleep:

Poo:

Times:

Activities

Weight   Height

Comments, (appearance, unusual smell, straining)

Behavior:

Comments (tiredness, hitting, biting, screaming etc.)

Date:

Food Eaten:

Parent/Carer

Breakfast _______________________________

Snack   _______________________________

Lunch   _______________________________

Snack   _______________________________

Dinner   _______________________________

Snack   _______________________________

Drinks:

1   2   3   4   5   6   7   8   9   10

Comments: supplements,(allergies e.t.c)

Sleep:

Awake:

Nap:

Asleep:

Activities

To do

I feel ...

Most enjoyable moment today...

Parent/carer & toddler activity for tomorrow

Date:

Toddler

Food Eaten:
Breakfast ____
Snack   ____
Lunch   ____
Snack   ____
Dinner   ____
Snack   ____

Drinks: 1   2   3   4   5   6   7   8

Comments: supplements,(allergies e.t.c)

Sleep: Activities
  Awake:
  Hours sleep last night:
  Nap:
  Asleep:
Poo:
                          Weight   Height
  Times:

Comments, (appearance, unusual smell, straining)

Behavior:

Comments (tiredness, hitting, biting, screaming etc.)

Date:

Food Eaten:

Breakfast ____

Snack _____________________________________

Lunch _____________________________________

Snack _____________________________________

Dinner _____________________________________

Snack _____________________________________

Drinks:

1   2   3   4   5   6   7   8   9   10

Comments: supplements.(allergies e.t.c)

Parent/Carer

Sleep:

Awake:

Nap:

Asleep:

Activities

To do

I feel ...

Most enjoyable moment today...

Parent/carer & toddler activity for tomorrow

Date: ☐   ⬭ Toddler ⬭

Food Eaten:
 Breakfast _______________________________________
 Snack   _______________________________________
 Lunch   _______________________________________
 Snack   _______________________________________
 Dinner   _______________________________________
 Snack   _______________________________________

 Drinks: 🥛 ☐ ☐ ☐ ☐ ☐ ☐ ☐
         1 2 3 4 5 6 7 8

Comments: supplements,(allergies e.t.c)

Sleep: Activities
 Awake:
 Hours sleep last night:
 Nap:
 Asleep:
 Poo:
                                    Weight   Height
   Times: ☐   ☐

Comments, (appearance, unusual smell, straining)

Behavior:

Comments (tiredness, hitting, biting, screaming etc.)

Date:

Food Eaten:

Breakfast _______________________________

Snack _______________________________

Lunch _______________________________

Snack _______________________________

Dinner _______________________________

Snack _______________________________

Drinks:

1   2   3   4   5   6   7   8   9   10

Comments: supplements,(allergies e.t.c)

Sleep:

Awake:

Nap:

Asleep:

Activities

To do

I feel ...

Most enjoyable moment today...

Parent/carer & toddler activity for tomorrow

Date: [ ] $\qquad$ **Toddler**

Food Eaten:

Breakfast ___________________________________

Snack   ___________________________________

Lunch   ___________________________________

Snack   ___________________________________

Dinner   ___________________________________

Snack   ___________________________________

Drinks: 1   2   3   4   5   6   7   8

Comments: supplements,(allergies e.t.c)

Sleep:

Awake:

Hours sleep last night:

Nap:

Asleep:

Poo:

Times: [ ] [ ] [ ]

Activities

Weight   Height

Comments, (appearance, unusual smell, straining,

Behavior:

Comments (tiredness, hitting, biting, screaming etc.)

Date:

Food Eaten:
Breakfast ___________________________________
Snack   ___________________________________
Lunch   ___________________________________
Snack   ___________________________________
Dinner   ___________________________________
Snack   ___________________________________

Drinks: 1   2   3   4   5   6   7   8   9   10

Comments: supplements,(allergies e.t.c)

Sleep:
Awake: Activities   To do
Nap:
Asleep:

I feel ...

Most enjoyable moment today...

Parent/carer & toddler activity for tomorrow

Date: _______ $\quad$ **Toddler**

Food Eaten:

Breakfast _________________________

Snack _________________________

Lunch _________________________

Snack _________________________

Dinner _________________________

Snack _________________________

Drinks: 1   2   3   4   5   6   7   8

Comments: supplements,(allergies e.t.c)

Sleep: Activities

Awake:

Hours sleep last night:

Nap:

Asleep:

Poo:

     Times: Weight   Height

Comments, (appearance, unusual smell, straining,

Behavior:

Comments (tiredness, hitting, biting, screaming etc.)

Date:

Food Eaten:

Breakfast ______________________________________

Snack ______________________________________

Lunch ______________________________________

Snack ______________________________________

Dinner ______________________________________

Snack ______________________________________

Drinks:

1   2   3   4   5   6   7   8   9   10

Parent/Carer

Comments: supplements,(allergies e.t.c)

Sleep:

Awake:

Nap:

Asleep:

Activities

To do

I feel ...

Most enjoyable moment today...

Parent/carer & toddler activity for tomorrow

Date: [ ]

Toddler

Food Eaten:

Breakfast _______________________________

Snack _______________________________

Lunch _______________________________

Snack _______________________________

Dinner _______________________________

Snack _______________________________

Drinks:

1 2 3 4 5 6 7 8

Comments: supplements,(allergies e.t.c)

Sleep:

Awake:

Hours sleep last night:

Nap:

Asleep:

Poo:

Times:

Activities

Weight   Height

Comments, (appearance, unusual smell, straining)

Behavior:

Comments (tiredness, hitting, biting, screaming etc.)

Date:

Parent/Carer

Food Eaten:
  Breakfast ________________________________
  Snack   ________________________________
  Lunch   ________________________________
  Snack   ________________________________
  Dinner   ________________________________
  Snack   ________________________________

Drinks:
          1   2   3   4   5   6   7   8   9   10

Comments: supplements,(allergies e.t.c)

Sleep:
  Awake:
  Nap:
  Asleep:

Activities

To do

I feel ...

Most enjoyable moment today...

Parent/carer & toddler activity for tomorrow

Date: [ ]

Toddler

Food Eaten:

Breakfast ________________________________

Snack   ________________________________

Lunch   ________________________________

Snack   ________________________________

Dinner   ________________________________

Snack   ________________________________

Drinks: 1   2   3   4   5   6   7   8

Comments: supplements,(allergies e.t.c)

Sleep:

  Awake: [ ]

  Hours sleep last night: [ ]

  Nap: [ ]

  Asleep: [ ]

  Poo:

    Times: [ ] [ ] [ ]

Activities

Weight [ ] Height [ ]

Comments, (appearance, unusual smell, straining)

Behavior:

Comments (tiredness, hitting, biting, screaming etc.)

Date:

Parent/Carer

Food Eaten:
Breakfast ____________________________
Snack ____________________________
Lunch ____________________________
Snack ____________________________
Dinner ____________________________
Snack ____________________________

Drinks:
1   2   3   4   5   6   7   8   9   10

Comments: supplements,(allergies e.t.c)

Sleep:
Awake:
Nap:
Asleep:

Activities

To do

I feel ...

Most enjoyable moment today...

Parent/carer & toddler activity for tomorrow

Date: [ ]

(Toddler)

Food Eaten:
Breakfast _______________________________
Snack   _______________________________
Lunch   _______________________________
Snack   _______________________________
Dinner   _______________________________
Snack   _______________________________

Drinks: 🥛 [ ] [ ] [ ] [ ] [ ] [ ] [ ]
        1   2   3   4   5   6   7   8

Comments: supplements,(allergies e.t.c)

Sleep: Activities
  Awake:
  Hours sleep last night:
  Nap:
  Asleep:
  Poo:
    Times: [ ] [ ] [ ]   Weight   Height

Comments, (appearance, unusual smell, straining,

Behavior:

Comments (tiredness, hitting, biting, screaming etc.)

Date:

Food Eaten:
    Breakfast _______________________________________
    Snack   _______________________________________
    Lunch   _______________________________________
    Snack   _______________________________________
    Dinner   _______________________________________
    Snack   _______________________________________

    Drinks:
              1   2   3   4   5   6   7   8   9   10

Comments: supplements,(allergies e.t.c)

Sleep:
    Awake:
    Nap:
    Asleep:

Activities

To do

I feel ...

Most enjoyable moment today...

Parent/carer & toddler activity for tomorrow

Date: [ ]

Toddler

Food Eaten:

Breakfast ___________________________

Snack   ___________________________

Lunch   ___________________________

Snack   ___________________________

Dinner   ___________________________

Snack   ___________________________

Drinks: [ ] [ ] [ ] [ ] [ ] [ ] [ ] [ ]
         1   2   3   4   5   6   7   8

Comments: supplements,(allergies e.t.c)

Sleep:

Awake:

Hours sleep last night:

Nap:

Asleep:

Poo:

Times:

Activities

Weight   Height

Comments, (appearance, unusual smell, straining)

Behavior:

Comments (tiredness, hitting, biting, screaming etc.)

Date:

Food Eaten:

Breakfast ______________________________

Snack ______________________________

Lunch ______________________________

Snack ______________________________

Dinner ______________________________

Snack ______________________________

Drinks:

1   2   3   4   5   6   7   8   9   10

Parent/Carer

Comments: supplements,(allergies e.t.c)

Sleep:

Awake:

Nap:

Asleep:

Activities

To do

I feel ...

Most enjoyable moment today...

Parent/carer & toddler activity for tomorrow

Date: 　　　 (Toddler)

Food Eaten:
Breakfast _______________________________________
Snack _______________________________________
Lunch _______________________________________
Snack _______________________________________
Dinner _______________________________________
Snack _______________________________________

Drinks: 1 2 3 4 5 6 7 8

Comments: supplements,(allergies e.t.c)

Sleep:
Awake:
Hours sleep last night:
Nap:
Asleep:
Poo:
Times:

Activities

Weight   Height

Comments, (appearance, unusual smell, straining,

Behavior:

Comments (tiredness, hitting, biting, screaming etc.)

Date:

Food Eaten:

Parent/Carer

    Breakfast _______________________________

    Snack   _______________________________

    Lunch   _______________________________

    Snack   _______________________________

    Dinner   _______________________________

    Snack   _______________________________

Drinks:

    1   2   3   4   5   6   7 8 9 10

Comments: supplements,(allergies e.t.c)

Sleep:

    Awake:

    Nap:

    Asleep:

Activities

To do

I feel ...

Most enjoyable moment today...

Parent/carer & toddler activity for tomorrow

Date: [ ]　　　　　　　　　　(Toddler)

Food Eaten:
  Breakfast ___________________________
  Snack   ___________________________
  Lunch   ___________________________
  Snack   ___________________________
  Dinner   ___________________________
  Snack   ___________________________

  Drinks: [glass]
            1   2   3   4   5   6   7   8

Comments: supplements,(allergies e.t.c)

Sleep: Activities
  Awake:
  Hours sleep last night:
  Nap:
  Asleep:
  Poo:
    Times: [ ] [ ] [ ]   Weight   Height

Comments, (appearance, unusual smell, straining)

Behavior:

Comments (tiredness, hitting, biting, screaming etc.)

Date:

Food Eaten:
  Breakfast _______________________________________
  Snack   _______________________________________
  Lunch   _______________________________________
  Snack   _______________________________________
  Dinner   _______________________________________
  Snack   _______________________________________

  Drinks:
            1   2   3   4   5   6   7   8   9   10

Comments: supplements,(allergies e.t.c)

Parent/Carer

Sleep:
  Awake:
  Nap:
  Asleep:

Activities

To do

I feel ...

Most enjoyable moment today...

Parent/carer & toddler activity for tomorrow

Date: ___________   Toddler

Food Eaten:
  Breakfast ________________________________
  Snack   ________________________________
  Lunch   ________________________________
  Snack   ________________________________
  Dinner   ________________________________
  Snack   ________________________________

  Drinks: 1   2   3   4   5   6   7   8

Comments: supplements,(allergies e.t.c)

Sleep: Activities
  Awake:
  Hours sleep last night:
  Nap:
  Asleep:
  Poo:
    Times: Weight   Height

Comments, (appearance, unusual smell, straining)

Behavior:

Comments (tiredness, hitting, biting, screaming etc.)

Date:

Food Eaten:

Breakfast __________________________________

Snack __________________________________

Lunch __________________________________

Snack __________________________________

Dinner __________________________________

Snack __________________________________

Drinks:

1   2   3   4   5   6   7   8   9   10

Comments: supplements,(allergies e.t.c)

Parent/Carer

Sleep:

Awake:

Nap:

Asleep:

Activities

To do

I feel ...

Most enjoyable moment today...

Parent/carer & toddler activity for tomorrow

Date: ____________ (Toddler)

Food Eaten:
 Breakfast ____
 Snack   ____
 Lunch   ____
 Snack   ____
 Dinner   ____
 Snack   ____

 Drinks: 1 2 3 4 5 6 7 8

Comments: supplements,(allergies e.t.c)

Sleep: Activities
 Awake:
 Hours sleep last night:
 Nap:
 Asleep:
 Poo:
   Times: Weight   Height

Comments, (appearance, unusual smell, straining)

Behavior:

Comments (tiredness, hitting, biting, screaming etc.)

Date:

Food Eaten:

Breakfast ___________________________________

Snack _______________________________________

Lunch _______________________________________

Snack _______________________________________

Dinner ______________________________________

Snack _______________________________________

Drinks:

1   2   3   4   5   6   7   8   9   10

Comments: supplements,(allergies e.t.c)

Sleep:

Awake:

Nap:

Asleep:

Activities

To do

I feel ...

Most enjoyable moment today...

Parent/carer & toddler activity for tomorrow

Parent/Carer

Date: [ ]

Toddler

Food Eaten:

Breakfast ______________________________

Snack ______________________________

Lunch ______________________________

Snack ______________________________

Dinner ______________________________

Snack ______________________________

Drinks: 1   2   3   4   5   6   7   8

Comments: supplements,(allergies e.t.c)

Sleep:

Awake:

Hours sleep last night:

Nap:

Asleep:

Poo:

Times:

Activities

Weight

Height

Comments, (appearance, unusual smell, straining)

Behavior:

Comments (tiredness, hitting, biting, screaming etc.)

Date:

Parent/Carer

Food Eaten:

Breakfast _______________________________________

Snack _______________________________________

Lunch _______________________________________

Snack _______________________________________

Dinner _______________________________________

Snack _______________________________________

Drinks:

1   2   3   4   5   6   7   8   9   10

Comments: supplements,(allergies e.t.c)

Sleep:

Awake:

Nap:

Asleep:

Activities

To do

I feel ...

Most enjoyable moment today...

Parent/carer & toddler activity for tomorrow

Date:

Toddler

Food Eaten:

Breakfast ______________________________________

Snack ______________________________________

Lunch ______________________________________

Snack ______________________________________

Dinner ______________________________________

Snack ______________________________________

Drinks:

1   2   3   4   5   6   7   8

Comments: supplements,(allergies e.t.c)

Sleep:

Awake:

Hours sleep last night:

Nap:

Asleep:

Poo:

Times:

Activities

Weight

Height

Comments, (appearance, unusual smell, straining)

Behavior:

Comments (tiredness, hitting, biting, screaming etc.)

Date:

Food Eaten:

Breakfast _______________________________

Snack   _______________________________

Lunch   _______________________________

Snack   _______________________________

Dinner   _______________________________

Snack   _______________________________

Drinks:

    1   2   3   4   5   6   7   8   9   10

Parent/Carer

Comments: supplements,(allergies e.t.c)

Sleep:

Awake:

Nap:

Asleep:

Activities

To do

I feel ...

Most enjoyable moment today...

Parent/carer & toddler activity for tomorrow

Date: ☐   (Toddler)

Food Eaten:

Breakfast ___________________________________

Snack   ___________________________________

Lunch   ___________________________________

Snack   ___________________________________

Dinner   ___________________________________

Snack   ___________________________________

Drinks: ☐
         1   2   3   4   5   6   7   8

Comments: supplements,(allergies e.t.c)

Sleep: Activities

Awake:

Hours sleep last night:

Nap:

Asleep:

Poo:
                          Weight   Height
   Times: ☐   ☐   ☐

Comments, (appearance, unusual smell, straining)

Behavior:

Comments (tiredness, hitting, biting, screaming etc.)

Date:

Parent/Carer

Food Eaten:
   Breakfast ____
   Snack   ____
   Lunch   ____
   Snack   ____
   Dinner   ____
   Snack   ____

Drinks:
        1   2   3   4   5   6   7 8 9 10

Comments: supplements,(allergies e.t.c)

Sleep:
   Awake:
   Nap:
   Asleep:

Activities

To do

I feel ...

Most enjoyable moment today...

Parent/carer & toddler activity for tomorrow

Date: [ ]

Food Eaten:

Breakfast ___________________________
Snack   ___________________________
Lunch   ___________________________
Snack   ___________________________
Dinner   ___________________________
Snack   ___________________________

Drinks: 1 2 3 4 5 6 7 8

Comments: supplements,(allergies e.t.c)

Sleep: Activities
  Awake:
  Hours sleep last night:
  Nap:
  Asleep:
  Poo:
                                      Weight   Height
    Times:

Comments, (appearance, unusual smell, straining)

Behavior:

Comments (tiredness, hitting, biting, screaming etc.)

Date:

Parent/Carer

Food Eaten:
   Breakfast __________________________
   Snack   __________________________
   Lunch   __________________________
   Snack   __________________________
   Dinner   __________________________
   Snack   __________________________

Drinks:
       1   2   3   4   5   6   7   8   9 10

Comments: supplements,(allergies e.t.c)

Sleep:
   Awake:
   Nap:
   Asleep:

Activities

To do

I feel ...

Most enjoyable moment today...

Parent/carer & toddler activity for tomorrow

Date:

Toddler

Food Eaten:

Breakfast ____

Snack   ____

Lunch   ____

Snack   ____

Dinner   ____

Snack   ____

Drinks: 1   2   3   4   5   6   7   8

Comments: supplements,(allergies e.t.c)

Sleep:

Awake:

Hours sleep last night:

Nap:

Asleep:

Poo:

Times:

Activities

Weight   Height

Comments, (appearance, unusual smell, straining)

Behavior:

Comments (tiredness, hitting, biting, screaming etc.)

Date:

Parent/Carer

Food Eaten:
Breakfast _______________________________________
Snack   _______________________________________
Lunch   _______________________________________
Snack   _______________________________________
Dinner   _______________________________________
Snack   _______________________________________

Drinks: 1   2   3   4   5   6   7   8   9   10

Comments: supplements,(allergies e.t.c)

Sleep:
Awake:
Nap:
Asleep:

Activities

To do

I feel ...

Most enjoyable moment today...

Parent/carer & toddler activity for tomorrow

Date: ⬚   (Toddler)

Food Eaten:

Breakfast ____

Snack   ____

Lunch   ____

Snack   ____

Dinner   ____

Snack   ____

Drinks: 🥛 ⬚ ⬚ ⬚ ⬚ ⬚ ⬚ ⬚ ⬚
             1   2   3   4   5   6   7   8

Comments: supplements,(allergies e.t.c)

Sleep: **Activities**

Awake:

Hours sleep last night:

Nap:

Asleep:

Poo: | Weight | Height |

   Times:

Comments, (appearance, unusual smell, straining)

Behavior:

Comments (tiredness, hitting, biting, screaming etc.)

Date:

Food Eaten:
Breakfast _______________________
Snack _______________________
Lunch _______________________
Snack _______________________
Dinner _______________________
Snack _______________________

Drinks:

1   2   3   4   5   6   7   8   9   10

Comments: supplements,(allergies e.t.c)

Parent/Carer

Sleep:
Awake:
Nap:
Asleep:

Activities

To do

I feel ...

Most enjoyable moment today...

Parent/carer & toddler activity for tomorrow

Date: [ ]   Toddler

Food Eaten:

Breakfast _______________________________

Snack _______________________________

Lunch _______________________________

Snack _______________________________

Dinner _______________________________

Snack _______________________________

Drinks: 1   2   3   4   5   6   7   8

Comments: supplements,(allergies e.t.c)

Sleep: Activities

Awake:

Hours sleep last night:

Nap:

Asleep:

Poo:

Times: [ ] [ ] [ ]   Weight   Height

Comments, (appearance, unusual smell, straining)

Behavior:

Comments (tiredness, hitting, biting, screaming etc.)

Date: _______

Toddler

Food Eaten:

Breakfast ________________________________

Snack   ________________________________

Lunch   ________________________________

Snack   ________________________________

Dinner   ________________________________

Snack   ________________________________

Drinks: 1   2   3   4   5   6   7   8

Comments: supplements,(allergies e.t.c)

Sleep:

Awake:

Hours sleep last night:

Nap:

Asleep:

Poo:

Times:

Activities

Weight   Height

Comments, (appearance, unusual smell, straining)

Behavior:

Comments (tiredness, hitting, biting, screaming etc.)

Date:

Parent/Carer

Food Eaten:
Breakfast _______________________________
Snack   _______________________________
Lunch   _______________________________
Snack   _______________________________
Dinner   _______________________________
Snack   _______________________________

Drinks: 1 2 3 4 5 6 7 8 9 10

Comments: supplements,(allergies e.t.c)

Sleep:
Awake:
Nap:
Asleep:

Activities

To do

I feel ...

Most enjoyable moment today...

Parent/carer & toddler activity for tomorrow

Date: [ ]

Toddler

Food Eaten:

Breakfast _________________________________

Snack _________________________________

Lunch _________________________________

Snack _________________________________

Dinner _________________________________

Snack _________________________________

Drinks: 1   2   3   4   5   6   7   8

Comments: supplements,(allergies e.t.c)

Sleep:

Awake:

Hours sleep last night:

Nap:

Asleep:

Poo:

Times:

Activities

Weight   Height

Comments, (appearance, unusual smell, straining)

Behavior:

Comments (tiredness, hitting, biting, screaming etc.)

Date:

Food Eaten:

Breakfast ____

Snack ____

Lunch ____

Snack ____

Dinner ____

Snack ____

Parent/Carer

Drinks:

1   2   3   4   5   6   7   8   9   10

Comments: supplements,(allergies e.t.c)

Sleep:

Awake:

Nap:

Asleep:

Activities

To do

I feel ...

Most enjoyable moment today...

Parent/carer & toddler activity for tomorrow

Date: [ ]   (Toddler)

Food Eaten:
Breakfast _______________________________
Snack   _______________________________
Lunch   _______________________________
Snack   _______________________________
Dinner   _______________________________
Snack   _______________________________

Drinks: 1   2   3   4   5   6   7   8

Comments: supplements,(allergies e.t.c)

Sleep: Activities
 Awake:
 Hours sleep last night:
 Nap:
 Asleep:
 Poo:
                          Weight   Height
   Times:

Comments, (appearance, unusual smell, straining)

Behavior:

Comments (tiredness, hitting, biting, screaming etc.)

Date:

Parent/Carer

Food Eaten:
    Breakfast _______________________________________
    Snack   _______________________________________
    Lunch   _______________________________________
    Snack   _______________________________________
    Dinner   _______________________________________
    Snack   _______________________________________

Drinks: 1   2   3   4   5   6   7   8   9   10

Comments: supplements,(allergies e.t.c)

Sleep:
    Awake:
    Nap:
    Asleep:

Activities

To do

I feel ...

Most enjoyable moment today...

Parent/carer & toddler activity for tomorrow

Date: 　　　　　　　　　　　　　Toddler

Food Eaten:

Breakfast ___________________________________

Snack　　___________________________________

Lunch　　___________________________________

Snack　　___________________________________

Dinner　　___________________________________

Snack　　___________________________________

Drinks:　　　1　2　3　4　5　6　7　8

Comments: supplements,(allergies e.t.c)

Sleep:　　　　　　　　　　　　　Activities

Awake:

Hours sleep last night:

Nap:

Asleep:

Poo:
　　　　　　　　　　　　Weight　　　Height
Times:

Comments, (appearance, unusual smell, straining)

Behavior:

Comments (tiredness, hitting, biting, screaming etc.)

Date:

Parent/Carer

Food Eaten:
   Breakfast _______________________________
   Snack   _______________________________
   Lunch   _______________________________
   Snack   _______________________________
   Dinner   _______________________________
   Snack   _______________________________

Drinks: 1   2   3   4   5   6   7   8   9   10

Comments: supplements,(allergies e.t.c)

Sleep:
   Awake:
   Nap:
   Asleep:

Activities

To do

I feel ...

Most enjoyable moment today...

Parent/carer & toddler activity for tomorrow

Date:

Toddler

Food Eaten:
  Breakfast ____
  Snack   ____
  Lunch   ____
  Snack   ____
  Dinner   ____
  Snack   ____

  Drinks: 1   2   3   4   5   6   7   8

Comments: supplements,(allergies e.t.c)

Sleep: Activities
  Awake:
  Hours sleep last night:
  Nap:
  Asleep:
Poo:
  Times: Weight   Height

Comments, (appearance, unusual smell, straining)

Behavior:

Comments (tiredness, hitting, biting, screaming etc.)

Date:

Parent/Carer

Food Eaten:
  Breakfast ___________________________
  Snack   ___________________________
  Lunch   ___________________________
  Snack   ___________________________
  Dinner   ___________________________
  Snack   ___________________________

Drinks: 1 2 3 4 5 6 7 8 9 10

Comments: supplements,(allergies e.t.c)

Sleep:
  Awake:
  Nap:
  Asleep:

Activities

To do

I feel ...

Most enjoyable moment today...

Parent/carer & toddler activity for tomorrow

Date: [ ]

(Toddler)

Food Eaten:

Breakfast ____

Snack   ____

Lunch   ____

Snack   ____

Dinner   ____

Snack   ____

Drinks: 1   2   3   4   5   6   7   8

Comments: supplements,(allergies e.t.c)

Sleep: Activities

  Awake:

  Hours sleep last night:

  Nap:

  Asleep:

  Poo:
                              Weight   Height
    Times:

Comments, (appearance, unusual smell, straining)

Behavior:

Comments (tiredness, hitting, biting, screaming etc.)

Date:

Parent/Carer

Food Eaten:
  Breakfast _______________________________________
  Snack   _______________________________________
  Lunch   _______________________________________
  Snack   _______________________________________
  Dinner   _______________________________________
  Snack   _______________________________________

Drinks: 1   2   3   4   5   6   7   8   9   10

Comments: supplements,(allergies e.t.c)

Sleep: Activities   To do
  Awake:
  Nap:
  Asleep:

  I feel ...

Most enjoyable moment today...

Parent/carer & toddler activity for tomorrow

Date:

Parent/Carer

Food Eaten:

Breakfast ___________________________________

Snack ___________________________________

Lunch ___________________________________

Snack ___________________________________

Dinner ___________________________________

Snack ___________________________________

Drinks:

1   2   3   4   5   6   7   8   9   10

Comments: supplements,(allergies e.t.c)

Sleep:

Awake:

Nap:

Asleep:

Activities

To do

I feel ...

Most enjoyable moment today...

Parent/carer & toddler activity for tomorrow

Date:

Parent/Carer

Food Eaten:
  Breakfast _______________________________
  Snack   _______________________________
  Lunch   _______________________________
  Snack   _______________________________
  Dinner   _______________________________
  Snack   _______________________________

Drinks: 1   2   3   4   5   6   7   8   9   10

Comments: supplements,(allergies e.t.c)

Sleep:
  Awake: Activities   To do
  Nap:
  Asleep:

I feel ...

Most enjoyable moment today...

Parent/carer & toddler activity for tomorrow

www.ingramcontent.com/pod-product-compliance
Lightning Source LLC
Chambersburg PA
CBHW050050260726

48658CB00005B/1871